MIGHTY MACHINES

Dump Trucks

by Ray McClellan

BLASTOFF! READERS

BELLWETHER MEDIA • MINNEAPOLIS, MN

Note to Librarians, Teachers, and Parents:

Blastoff! Readers are carefully developed by literacy experts and combine standards-based content with developmentally appropriate text.

Level 1 provides the most support through repetition of high-frequency words, light text, predictable sentence patterns, and strong visual support.

Level 2 offers early readers a bit more challenge through varied simple sentences, increased text load, and less repetition of high-frequency words.

Level 3 advances early-fluent readers toward fluency through increased text and concept load, less reliance on visuals, longer sentences, and more literary language.

Whichever book is right for your reader, Blastoff! Readers are the perfect books to build confidence and encourage a love of reading that will last a lifetime!

This edition first published in 2007 by Bellwether Media.

No part of this publication may be reproduced in whole or in part without written permission of the publisher. For information regarding permission, write to Bellwether Media Inc., Attention: Permissions Department, Post Office Box 1C, Minnetonka, MN 55345-9998.

Library of Congress Cataloging-in-Publication Data
McClellan, Ray.
 Dump trucks / by Ray McClellan.
  p. cm. — (Blastoff! readers) (Mighty machines)
Summary: "Simple text and supportive images introduce young readers to dump trucks. Intended for students in kindergarten through third grade."
 Includes bibliographical references and index.
 ISBN-10: 1-60014-046-7 (hardcover : alk. paper)
 ISBN-13: 978-1-60014-046-4 (hardcover : alk. paper)
 1. Dump trucks—Juvenile literature. 2. Earthwork—Juvenile liteature. I. Title. II. Series. III. Series: Mighty machines (Bellwether Media)

TL230.15.M425 2007
 624.1'52—dc22   2006007214

Table of Contents

The dump truck
is a big machine.
It can carry
heavy **loads**.

The dump truck has a **cab**. A worker sits in the cab.

cab

The dump truck
has big tires.

tires

The dump
truck has
a **box**.

box

This machine
loads the
box of the
dump truck.

13

Dump trucks carry dirt, sand, and rocks.

The box tips to dump its load.

The load falls
to the ground.

19

The dump truck
drives away
to pick up
another load.

Glossary

box—the back end of a dump truck; the box holds the load.

cab—the place where the driver sits

load—anything that is carried or lifted by a machine or a person

To Learn More

AT THE LIBRARY

Bridges, Sara. *I Drive a Dump Truck*. Mankato, Minn.: Picture Window Books, 2004.

Jango-Cohen, Judith. *Dump Trucks*. Minneapolis, Minn.: Lerner, 2003.

Randolph, Joanne. *Dump Trucks*. New York: Powerkids Press, 2002.

ON THE WEB

Learning more about mighty machines is as easy as 1, 2, 3.

1. Go to www.factsurfer.com

2. Enter "mighty machines" into search box.

3. Click the "Surf" button and you will see a list of related web sites.

With factsurfer.com, finding more information is just a click away.

Index

The photographs in this book are reproduced with the permission of: Deere, Inc., front cover, pp. 4-5, 12-13, 16-17, 20-21; The Volvo Group, pp. 6-7, 10-11, 14-15, 18-19; Tony Tremblay, pp. 8-9.